STEVE PARISH

Discover & learn about
Australian
Coasts
AND OCEANS

Text Pat Slater

Photographs Steve Parish

HABITATS & ECOSYSTEMS

Contents

see page 7

see page 16

see page 40

The voyage of Ark Australia

About 160 million years ago, the world continent called Pangea split into two supercontinents, Laurasia and Gondwana.

By 70 million years ago, India, New Zealand and South America had broken from Gondwana, leaving Antarctica and Australia behind. By 40 million years ago, Australia was drifting northwards alone. Like a giant Noah's Ark, it carried a cargo of living things.

As the giant landmass moved slowly through the ocean, its landscapes and seascapes changed. Earth movements pushed up mountains. Low-lying areas became freshwater lakes or shallow seas. At some periods, when the water from the world's oceans was locked up as ice, sea level dropped and the coastline extended a long way. When the ice melted, the sea crept back, drowning river valleys and cutting off coastal mountains as islands. Australia's coastal and marine plants and animals were not so cut off from the rest of the world as were land plants and animals because new species could swim or drift to shore. Coastal and marine plant and animal communities[G] established themselves. As the north of the continent reached regions where the sea water was warmer, coral reefs and mangrove swamps grew around the coast.

Anemonefishes live with sea anemones, protected by their stinging tentacles.

Then, perhaps as much as 60 000 years ago, the ancestors of today's Aboriginal Australians crossed the narrowing sea from Asia. They quickly spread all over the continent, and those groups along the coastline lived well without harming the coastal habitats.

In 1788, European humans came on board Ark Australia, bringing a variety of animals with them. They cleared large parts of Australia and, in just over 200 years, great changes took place. Natural wetlands and waterways carried pollution[G] or salt into the ocean. The coasts were cleared, drained and settled. Agricultural chemicals and sewage entered the sea. Estuaries silted up, seagrass beds disappeared and marine resources were over-fished.

Gradually, Australians have realised that Ark Australia floats in an ocean whose resources must be saved. They hope that some of the damage to to the coast and marine systems can be repaired and that this will be part of a worldwide effort to protect the ocean.

This series of books describes the places where plants and animals live in Australia today – the habitats of Ark Australia. This volume is on the coasts and oceans of our wonderful continent.

Australians are still lucky enough to have stretches of coastline that have not been built on or polluted.

The mighty ocean

The ocean covers about 70% of the Earth's surface. It is made up of water in which are dissolved solid materials, including a large amount of salt. The upper layer of the ocean, which is only around 2% of its total volume[G], is warmed by the Sun and stirred by the wind. Water evaporates[G] from the ocean's surface, condenses[G] and falls again as rain. This rain falls on land and runs off into the ocean, carrying with it dissolved materials and solid matter.

Currents are rivers of water moving through the ocean.

Deep currents are caused by differences in water temperature. Cold water at the North and South Poles[G] sinks and moves through the depths toward the Equator[G]. Warm equatorial water flows over it toward the Poles.

Surface currents are pushed across the ocean by the winds that blow in patterns across the Earth.

Earth's climates[G] and weather[G] are influenced by ocean currents moving warm or cold water between different places. Wind blowing over a warm current will pick up more rain than if it blew over a cold current.

Tides and waves

A wave moves across the surface of the sea but does not carry water.

Tides are water movements caused by the gravitational[G] pull of the Moon on ocean water. As the Earth turns, twice daily the water below the Moon is sucked upwards, then sinks back again.

Waves are big ripples of surface water caused by the wind. The movement passes onwards, but the water itself does not flow far.

○ HOW THE OCEANS STAY SALTY ○

The heat of the Sun evaporates fresh water from the ocean.

Clouds of water vapour[G] are blown over the land. The vapour forms rain.

The rivers flow into the sea. The salt they carry is added to the sea water.

Rain falls. It carries salt from the land into streams and rivers.

FACTS 'N' FIGURES FILE

• **The words "ocean" and "sea"** mean the same thing. "Sea" may also mean a piece of ocean with land on most sides of it.

• **The sea appears blue** because red waves of light disappear in the water faster than do blue waves of light.

• **At the surface, a red fish appears red.** Below about 20 m it appears black, since no red light can reach that depth.

• **Only a tiny amount of light** travels down into the sea more than a few hundred metres. Past that, the water is dark.

• **The ocean is saltiest** where plenty of water enters it and evaporation is high.

• **Plants and animals** mostly live in the top layer of the ocean, because they need sunlight to make energy.

• **The distance the tide** rises and falls depends on how close the Earth is to the Moon and, to a lesser extent, the Sun.

• **The lowest layers** of the ocean are almost freezing cold.

• **The shape of the ocean floor** and the coastline also affect the rise and fall of the tide. In the Kimberley of Western Australia the difference between high and low tide levels may be 9 m.

Where ocean meets land

A coastline is the strip where the land ends and the sea begins. It is a meeting place between the terrestrial[G] world of land plants and animals and the marine[G] world of sea plants and animals.

The Australian mainland and Tasmania have a total coastline length of 36 700 km. This provides habitats for many plants and animals.

On the landward edge of a coastline are sandy dunes and coastal swamps. On the seaward side, the intertidal zone (the area between high and low tide) runs down to the subtidal zone (which is always below water).

MANY HABITATS IN ONE AREA

1 Coastal heath

2 Sand dunes

3 Sandy beach

4 Sandbar

5 Tidal creek

6 Estuary

7 Rocky headland

8 Intertidal zone

9 Rocky reef

10 Soft bottom

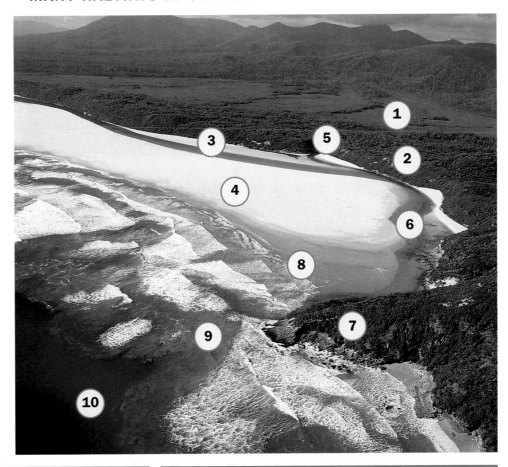

○ LENGTHS OF STATE COASTLINES ○

Western Australia	12 500 km
Queensland	7 400 km
Northern Territory	6 200 km
South Australia	3 700 km
Tasmania	3 200 km
New South Wales	1 900 km
Victoria	1 800 km
Australian Capital Territory	353 km

○ TIDAL TERMS, WAVY WORDS ○

High-tide mark	The level reached by the highest tides.
Low-tide mark	The level reached by the lowest tides.
Intertidal zone	The area between high and low tide marks.
Subtidal zone	The area below low tide mark.
Crest of a wave	The wave's highest point.
Trough of a wave	The wave's lowest point.
Height of a wave	The distance between a wave's crest and trough.

The ever-changing coast

What a coastline is like depends on a number of things:

- The materials it is made of, from hard rocks through softer rocks, stones and rubble[G] to sand or mud.

- The conformation[G] of the land, including headlands, bays, long sandy beaches, etc.
- The way in which the ocean breaks the coastline down and adds things to it.
- The actions and effects of living organisms[G].

WHAT COASTLINES ARE MADE OF

Hard rock such as granite.

Softer rock such as limestone.

Sand.

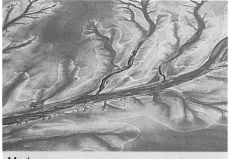
Mud.

Plants rooted in sand or mud.

Coral rubble and coral sand.

HOW HUMANS ALTER COASTLINES

Australians are shifting to the coast in ever-increasing numbers.

Humans like living beside the ocean. They want to enjoy themselves sailing, swimming, surfing and fishing. When they settle on a coastline, they want to keep beaches and do not want salty swamps and mudflats. They build jetties and groynes[G], bulldoze mangroves, fill in wetlands, spray insects with pesticides[G], and put up buildings along the seafront and for quite some distance inland from it. All these actions destroy habitats for many plants and animals. New habitats are created, but they are often poor in species compared to those that once were there.

The ocean at work

THE SEA CARVES THE COAST

The currents do not allow sand to settle on this wave-worn rock.

Sand carried by the waves covers the rocky skeleton of this beach.

The waves carry sand and rocks that swirl and tumble, scouring away the shore. Then the back flow drags the debris^G back to sea. Currents carry it and drop it somewhere else on the coast. The appearance of a beach depends on the material it is made of and the ways in which waves and wind act on it.

As a wave breaks over rocks, water is forced into cracks, making them wider.

As the water runs back, it sucks on the rock, further weakening it.

Stones in a rock hole swirl around with each wave, making the hole larger.

ON THE BEACH

A beach is a ribbon of sand (or stones, shells or mud) that lies along the edge of the water. The sea is constantly picking up material from a beach, carrying it somewhere else, then dropping it. The sand or other material that forms beaches originally comes from eroded^G sea cliffs or has been carried to the coast by rivers.

A north-western beach of red sand.

Eroded cliffs and dunes supply sand and other materials for beaches.

Coastal and ocean habitats

Dunes and beaches.

Sandflats and mudflats.

Estuaries.

Mangroves and salt marshes.

Soft bottom habitats.

Seagrass beds and seaweeds.

Intertidal zones.

Rocky reefs and continental islands.

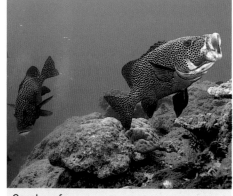

Coral reefs.

Coral cays and islands.

The open sea.

Australia's coastline

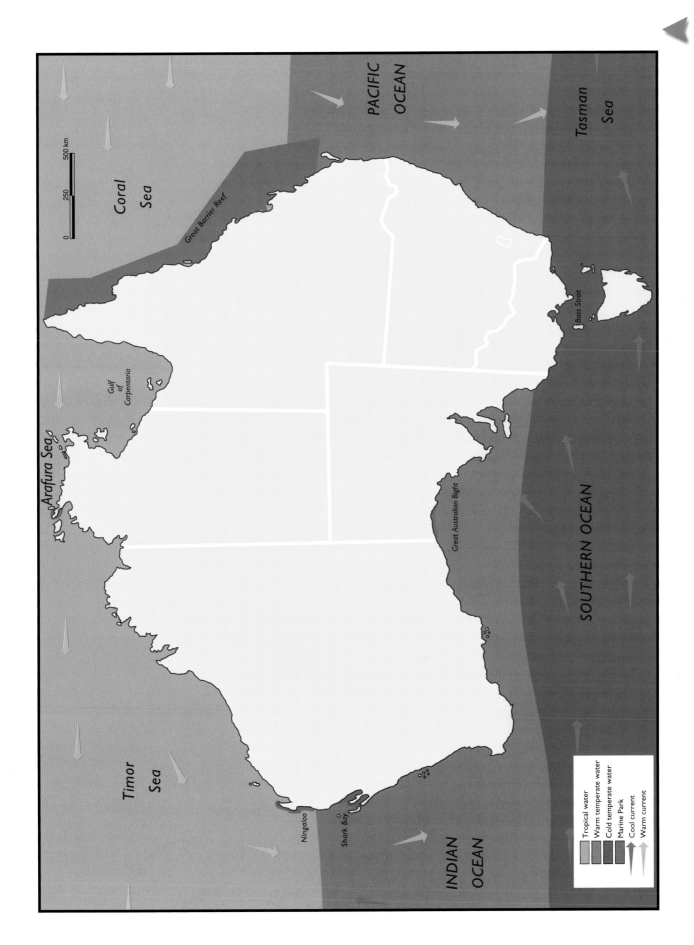

PACIFIC OCEAN

Tasman Sea

Coral Sea

500 km
250
0

Great Barrier Reef

Bass Strait

Gulf of Carpentaria

Arafura Sea

Great Australian Bight

SOUTHERN OCEAN

Timor Sea

Ningaloo

Shark Bay

INDIAN OCEAN

Tropical water
Warm temperate water
Cold temperate water
Marine Park
Cool current
Warm current

Coastal plants

Fresh water is often scarce on the seashore. Coastal plants are adapted[G] to dry conditions in the same ways as are desert plants. Their leaves are small or hairy or tough on the surface, and allow little water to escape. Coastal plants may have fleshy leaves or stems that store water.

The soil in which coastal plants grow is often salty. Some seashore plants filter[G] salt out of the water they take in through their roots. They may also store salt in their leaves, then drop the leaves.

Winds from the sea, which can be gale-force and often carry salt spray, blow over coastal plants. Often these plants grow close to the ground, to avoid the full force of gales. They have strong root systems to anchor them.

Some taller plants, such as pandanus and coconut palms, have roots that prop them up and hold them in place.

○ POWERED BY THE SUN ○

Chlorophyll makes the leaves of these plants green.

The cells[G] of all plants contain a green substance called chlorophyll. This allows the plant to make use of sunshine to power food-making in a process called photosynthesis.

The raw materials a plant needs to make food include water, nitrogen and carbon. The nitrogen, mixed with water, is taken in by the plant's roots. Carbon dioxide is taken from the air. During photosynthesis, the carbon is used and oxygen passes out of the plant. This is known as gas exchange.

○ COASTAL HEATH PLANTS ○

The area on the landward side of beaches and dunes is often a coastal heath. This is an area with sandy soil that is not rich in plant foods. In springtime, many heathland plants are covered in flowers. These often contain nectar[G]. The pollen[G] from these flowers is carried to other flowers by nectar-eating animals such as moths, wasps, birds and mammals[G].

Coastal heathland plants.

DRIFTERS

Coconuts may grow from drifted seeds.

Beach-drifted coconut.

The fruits and seeds of some coastal plants can survive while floating in salt water. They drift on the ocean currents. When they wash up on new shores, they put down roots and grow.

Pandanus with fruits.

Dune and beach plants

HOLDING DOWN THE SHORELINE

GRASSES

Coastal grasses spread over sand, anchoring it. If sand buries one part of the plant, another keeps growing.

CREEPERS

Creepers are pioneer^G beach plants. They may grow right down to the high-tide line.

SUCCULENTS

Some beach plants store water in thick, fleshy leaves or stems. Hairy or waxy surfaces protect their leaves.

SHE-OAKS

She-oaks (casuarinas) tolerate wet and salty soil. They are found on front-line sand dunes.

PANDANUS

Pandanus has saw-edged leaves that screw around a central stem. Prop roots anchor a tree in the sand.

SHRUBS

Many sand-dune shrubs grow close to the ground. This protects them from the sea winds.

FACTS 'N' FIGURES FILE

- **Plants make the oxygen** that animals need for survival.

- **The soil of coastal heathlands** is often poor in plant nutrients. Some heathland plants have fungus living on their roots that helps them make use of what food material there is.

- **Coastal heaths and swamps** may have local names. In south-eastern Queensland this country is called the Wallum.

- **Coastal heaths** in south-western WA are

home to endangered^G animals, including the Noisy Scrub-bird, the Western Whipbird and the Long-nosed Potoroo.

- **Seeds from beach plants** can be found in the flotsam^G washed up on a beach. They form food for beach animals.

- **Coconut palms** were introduced^G to Australian coasts. Their drifted seeds have made them common on northern shores.

- **As beach plants grow**, they drop leaves that break down to form plant food. The

soil becomes richer and can hold more water. Woodland plants move in and take over the area.

- **Sand dune plants** can be destroyed by storms, droughts, fire, clearing by humans, grazing by animals, or too much wear from human feet or vehicles.

- **When sand dune plants disappear**, the dune is blown inland by the sea wind. When it goes, there is no reservoir of sand to protect the beach from erosion.

Phytoplankton and seagrasses

Phytoplankton are tiny, single-celled plants. The base of all ocean food-chains, they drift in ocean currents and are thickest where plant nutrients[G] are richest. Many of these nutrients come to the ocean's surface on currents of water rising from the depths.

Phytoplankton are eaten by tiny, single-celled animals (zooplankton). Both phytoplankton and zooplankton are eaten by larger creatures. They form the smallest links in the chain that leads to creatures as huge as the baleen[G] whales.

Seagrasses are related to land grasses. They have strap-like leaves with veins running side by side. These leaves grow from runners called rhizomes, which have roots growing into the seabed.

Seagrasses grow on soft sea-bottoms in sheltered bays and estuaries. They are eaten by some large animals, including marine turtles and the Dugong. However, many smaller animals in seagrass beds do not eat the seagrasses. Instead, they feed on the plants and animals growing on the seagrass leaves.

Seagrass beds are vulnerable[G] to pollution.

○ TINY MUDFLAT PLANTS ○

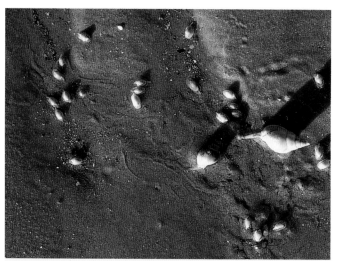

These molluscs[G] are grazing on tiny plants on the mud.

○ SEAGRASSES ○

Flutemouths and other fishes live in seagrass beds.

MANGROVES

Mangrove trees grow in tidal areas, some where their roots and lower trunks are regularly submerged. They put up special aerating roots that take in oxygen. Their root systems anchor them and hold the sediment[G] around them in place. Mangroves provide habitat for many animals. Some, such as insects, spiders and molluscs, live on the trunks and in the leaves. Others, such as crabs, shrimps, worms and fish fry, live in the water and mud amongst the roots.

In a mangrove swamp. The roots poking above the sand take in oxygen.

Marine algae – the seaweeds

Seaweeds are large algae[G]. They have simple structures that are not true leaves, stems or roots, and they fasten themselves to hard surfaces using discs called "holdfasts". They carry out photosynthesis and need sunlight to grow.

Blue-green algae is a primitive[G] seaweed that looks like slime. It covers rocks just above the high-tide line along rocky shores. Other sorts of seaweeds are divided into green, brown and red according to their colour. They may grow as strands, or fronds, or in branches, or as a crust that looks like paint.

Seaweeds have high food value and are eaten by many grazing creatures.

SEAWEEDS

Seaweeds use holdfasts to cling to hard surfaces.

Seaweeds form habitat for a variety of marine creatures.

Australian Fur-seals in giant kelp. Inset: A buoyancy bladder.

FACTS 'N' FIGURES FILE

- **Plant life can grow only** where light passes through the water. This ranges from depths of 200 m in the clearest ocean water to around 30 m along the coast and less than 5 m in estuaries.

- **The sea appears green** when the surface layers are full of phytoplankton.

- **The total weight** of all the phytoplankton produced in the sea in one year is far more than the weight of all the fishes.

- **Single-celled plants** double their numbers each day when conditions are good.

- **Phytoplankton make up around 33%** of all plant tissue produced on Earth.

- **"Red tides"** that can kill marine life are caused by single-celled algae undergoing a population explosion.

- **Australia has about 35** species of seagrasses. The largest areas are off the coasts of Western and South Australia.

- **Seagrasses existed 70 million** years ago, before the break-up of Gondwana.

- **Algae take in food materials** and oxygen from the water through their surface. Many-celled algae, such as seaweeds, have to grow as sheets or strands only a few cells thick.

- **Southern Australia** has about 1300 species of seaweeds.

- **Giant kelp** may grow over 0.3 m in a day. The tip of a frond may be 45 m from the holdfast on the ocean floor. Each frond contains buoyancy bladders – these keep it floating upward.

Animals above high-tide line

All animals need air to breathe, water and food. They need ways of sheltering from too much heat and cold, ways of protecting themselves against predators[G] and conditions in which they can breed safely.

The coast and the ocean provide many different types of habitat for animals, from the coastal heaths and dune systems down the rocky, sandy or muddy beach into the water and out to sea.

Within each of these habitats there will be micro-habitats. For example, on a rocky beach, animals may live in cracks between rocks, or on rock surfaces, or in tidal pools, or in the sand that is washed into gaps between rocks.

They may live at different levels, from the highest, which is only splashed by water at very high tides, down to the sub-tidal zone, which is always under water.

COASTAL HEATH AND SWAMP CREATURES

Animals that live in coastal heaths find protection in the low, often thick, bushes and tangled undergrowth. The coastal creeks and swamps are also rich in fauna[G]. In springtime, when heathland plants flower, birds, mammals and insects can be found in this habitat in large numbers.

Some rare birds and mammals are found in coastal heaths and swamps. These areas are vulnerable to fire and to clearing by humans.

Small marsupials[G] live in the thick undergrowth in heath habitats.

Honeyeaters feed on the nectar in heathland flowers.

FACTS 'N' FIGURES FILE

- **Many shore animals feed**, rest and breed at particular stages of the tides. The incoming water brings food, oxygen and hiding places. However, it also brings predators and battering waves.

- **Tides influence the lives** of shore animals by altering the salinity, temperature and pressure of the water they live in.

- **The Little Penguin** is the world's smallest penguin. An adult weighs 1 kg, stands 40 cm tall and may live for 6 years.

- **A pair of Little Penguins** mates for life.

- **Land-living hermit crabs** have large gill chambers. These are kept moist and act as a type of lung. This lets the crabs live on land, but the females must still release their eggs into the sea.

- **The "crazy crabs"** sold in pet stores are land-living hermit crabs. In the wild, they scavenge[G] at night.

LIFE IN THE DUNES

Wading birds find food and shelter in lagoons and tidal creeks running through sand dunes.

Little Penguins nest in the dunes.

Insects leave tracks in the sand.

Crabs in the intertidal zone

Rock crabs live on rocky shores that are washed by high-energy waves. They shelter in crevices or cracks, sometimes clinging upside-down, and feed on algae growing on the rocks.

Fast-running ghost crabs live on sandy beaches, burrowing at high-tide level and in sand dunes. They are night-time predators on small creatures as well as being scavengers[G].

Hermit crabs have naked abdomens that they hide in mollusc shells. They can survive out of water for long periods, hide in burrows in the sand and scavenge at night.

Soldier crabs move in masses across tidal flats feeding on tidal debris. Unlike other crabs, they can run forwards. When the tide returns, they burrow into the sand.

The Mud Crab burrows into soft bottoms, especially mud in mangrove swamps. It emerges to feed when the tide floods the swamp. This species is fished commercially by humans.

Burrowing sand crabs live from the intertidal zone to the subtidal zone down to a depth of 60 m. They can swim but spend most of their time buried in the sand.

The intertidal zone is habitat for many different species of animals. A number of different types of crabs make the area from sand dunes to surf and the subtidal zone their home. They shelter, find food and escape from predators in a number of ways.

Shallow water animals

Many creatures live in the shallow parts of the ocean around Australia.

They make their homes in a variety of habitats, from cold southern estuaries to warm coral seas. They include many species of invertebrate[G] and vertebrate[G] animals.

An invertebrate animal has no backbone, skeleton or spinal cord of nerve tissue. Marine invertebrates include sponges, coelenterates[G], worms, molluscs, crustaceans[G], bryozoans[G], echinoderms[G] and ascidians[G].

A vertebrate animal has a backbone, a skeleton and a spinal cord of nerve tissue. Marine vertebrates include reptiles (crocodiles, sea snakes and turtles), fishes, birds and mammals (seals, dolphins, whales and the Dugong).

SOME MARINE INVERTEBRATES

Sponges.

Coelenterates.

Worm.

Crustacean.

Mollusc.

Bryozoan.

Echinoderm.

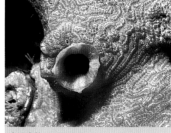
Ascidian.

SOME MARINE VERTEBRATES

Reptile.

Bird.

Fish.

Mammal.

Open water animals

Many sea creatures spend their young stages in sheltered inshore waters, even though, as adults, they live in deeper waters. This is why estuaries, mangrove swamps and bays are important nurseries for fish and other marine life. When the creatures are old enough to face the dangers of the open sea, they move there.

Open sea (or pelagic) fishes often live in schools. This protects them against predators. They return to shallow water to spawn^G. Many other vertebrates that feed in the open sea, such as birds, turtles and seals, return to land to breed. However, dolphins and whales cannot return to the land. They mate and give birth in the water.

SEALS, DOLPHINS AND WHALES

Australian Fur-seals.

Australian Sea-lion and pup.

Humpback Whale.

Bottlenose Dolphins.

Seals and sea-lions can move about on land. They come to shore to breed. However, dolphins and whales will die if beached. All marine mammals have thick layers of under-skin fat to keep them warm in the heat-draining sea.

PELAGIC FISHES

Tiny, plankton-eating fishes find shelter under a sea jelly.

Predatory fishes may hunt in packs.

In the open sea, hiding places are rare. Hunters and hunted are fast swimmers.

FACTS 'N' FIGURES FILE

- **Many open-water creatures** are counter-shaded, with dark topsides and paler undersides. This camouflages^G them from predators above and below.

- **The young stages, or larvae,** of many fishes look very different from the adults.

- **Pelagic fishes** are eaten by humans. Over-fishing threatens some species.

- **The Australian Sea-lion** was once killed

for oil from its fat. The population is now about 10 000 around southern coasts.

- **A female sea-lion** has one pup about every 18 months.

- **The Southern Right Whale** was hunted almost to extinction^G. Today there may be up to 4000. Some appear off southern Australian shores from May to December.

- **Where nutrients come** to the surface

from the deep sea, plankton grow well and form food for fishes.

- **The deeps of the ocean** are dark and cold. The bodies of surface creatures sink and provide some food for animals here.

- **Sea jellies eat plankton.** They grow and breed rapidly. Sometimes the total weight of sea jellies in an area far outweighs the total weight of all other creatures.

Beaches and dunes

A sandy beach is a sloping stretch of shoreline made up of sand grains.

This type of beach is most often found in a coastal area with moderate wave action. If the waves are severe, the sand washes away. If there is little wave action, the sloping beach is replaced by a sandflat. A beach may appear to be bare of animal life. However, many of the creatures that live there are tiny, or spend a lot of time buried under the sand. The waves constantly rearrange their habitat, eroding and reburying it. The water brings fresh oxygen and food supplies, as well as predators, to the beach.

A sandy beach may stretch inland in the form of sand dunes. These are formed of wind-blown sand piled into heaps and held down by dune grasses and shrubby plants. Sand dunes attract creatures from the land and from the beach. Many burrow for protection, while others visit the dunes at night.

BETWEEN THE LAND AND THE SEA

A long sandy beach may appear bare of animals but can hide many creatures.

Seaweed and other flotsam is eaten by beach grazers and scavengers.

A beach of shells.

Pellets of sand left where sand-bubbler crabs have been feeding.

Some beach-living animals hide in burrows during the day and come out onto the sand at night to feed. Others move through the food-rich surface layers of sand, following the tide as it moves in and out.

Food sources on beaches include phytoplankton, seaweeds and seagrasses that drift ashore, and detritus[G] and tiny algae growing on the sand. Predators eat the herbivores[G] and scavengers that feed on these things.

FACTS 'N' FIGURES FILE

- **Sixty-five per cent** of the coastline of southern Australia is sandy beach.
- **Beach sand grains** may range in size from coarse to fine. The beach may also contain pieces of shells, pebbles, etc.
- **Sandy beaches' height increases** in the south in summer and autumn when waves carry sand ashore. During winter storms, this extra sand is scooped back to sea.
- **Rocky headlands protect beaches** from very strong wave action.
- **A bar is an offshore ridge** of sand running parallel to a beach.
- **A rip is usually water** washing back to sea through gaps in a bar.
- **Beach litter** should be handled with care. Sharp, disease-carrying human rubbish may be found amongst flotsam.
- **Bivalve molluscs** such as cockles may surf up and down the beach with the waves. They filter-feed while covered with water. Then they bury themselves while the sand is still waterlogged after a wave.
- **Tiny crustaceans** called amphipods[G] feed on drifted seaweeds and seagrasses. They hop away when flotsam is shifted.
- **Sand dunes** are reservoirs of sand that may form new beaches after storms. Building houses on dunes removes this buffer[G] zone from the beach.

Beaches and dunes

ABOVE HIGH-WATER MARK

HOLDING DOWN THE DUNES

Grasses pioneer the dunes.

Creepers help fix the sand.

Shrubs and trees grow as nutrients in the soil build up.

DETECTING ON THE BEACH

The skeleton, or test, of a heart urchin.

Razor shells live in sand or mud. They anchor themselves narrow-end down.

A walk along a beach will reveal many things that have been washed ashore. This flotsam gives clues to the local marine life.

The cockle is a filter-feeder.

The rock lobster lives in crevices among reefs.

This turtle crawled up the beach to lay its eggs, then died or was killed there.

Egg mass of a snail-like mollusc.

Sea snakes are air-breathers. They are venomous and a stranded one should be left alone.

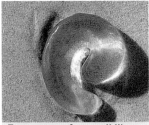

A sea jelly contains a lot of water. It melts away when stranded.

Sandflats and mudflats

A sandflat, or a mudflat, is a flat area of sandy or muddy seabed that is uncovered by low tide.

Around the coasts of northern Australia, where the tide rises and falls a great distance twice each 24 hours, there are many large tidal flats.

Around the coasts of southern Australia, where the tidal rise and fall is far less, only 5% of the shoreline is made up of sandflats or mudflats.

A tidal flat and the life forms on and in it are influenced by the tides and the sediment the water carries and drops.

The surface of a tidal flat is home to cyano-bacteria[G] and single-celled algae. These use the energy of the Sun, water and carbon dioxide to photosynthesise sugars and starches. The process releases oxygen. Other sorts of bacteria[G] use the oxygen to break down plant and animal material. So the tidal flat is like a large living thing itself, as well as being habitat for many other life forms.

EXPOSED BY LOW TIDE

A tidal flat is covered with sea water twice each day. When the tide ebbs, much of the flat is exposed to the air.

These channels will contain algae and other organic food for tidal flat creatures.

FACTS 'N' FIGURES FILE

• **Mud will pass** through a 0.063 mm mesh sieve. Sand grains are too large to pass through the mesh.

• **Bacteria working in mudflats** may release hydrogen sulphide and methane gases while breaking down organic chemicals. These are "rotten egg" gases.

• **The more oxygen** there is in a sandflat or mudflat, the faster bacteria work.

• **Ghost shrimps,** also called nippers, burrow through sediment when feeding. They pump water through their burrows, taking oxygen into the sediment.

• **Crabs and other scavengers** on tidal flats track down dead bodies by tasting chemicals released into the water.

• **Tidal flats take a long time** to recover from an oil spill. This is because the toxic[G] oil is trapped in the sediment and does not wash away.

• **Many tidal flat animals** will die when very low tides expose the flat for long periods on hot summer days.

• **Different species of wading** shorebirds have beaks of different lengths. They can take different prey from the same place.

• **The Mudskipper is a fish** that walks over mud on leg-like fins. It breathes oxygen taken from the water it carries in pouches surrounding its gills.

Sandflats and mudflats

INTERTIDAL PLAINS

FLAT MATES

Wading shorebirds dig their beaks into the sand or mud to find small prey.

The animals that burrow into an intertidal flat move the surface about. They shovel it out of their burrow, or they eat it, digest the food material and excrete[G] the waste. Larger predators, such as wading birds, hunt the buried creatures.

Shrimps burrow into the tidal flat.

The heart urchin uses its spines to burrow.

ALGAL GRAZERS

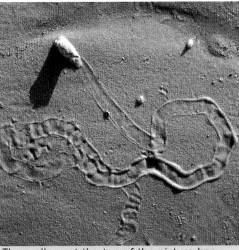

The mollusc at the top of the picture has left a trail as it grazes algae.

The surface of an intertidal flat is coated by a fine layer of microscopic[G] plants. These are eaten by grazing molluscs, and by crustaceans such as soldier crabs.

DINING WITH THE TURNING TIDE

The oystercatcher opens bivalve molluscs with its chisel-like beak.

When the tide is out, animals of the tidal flat come out of their burrows to feed. As the tide returns, filter-feeders such as bivalve molluscs open to take in water. Predators such as toadfish, stingrays and sharks swim in with the tide to hunt.

Wading birds search the tidal flat for food, finding creatures by probing into the mud or sand with their long beaks.

A Mudskipper takes to land, its gill pouches bulging with water.

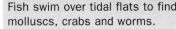

Fish swim over tidal flats to find molluscs, crabs and worms.

Stingrays can enter very shallow water to hunt for molluscs.

Bivalve molluscs open their shells to filter-feed.

Estuaries

An estuary is a body of water that has connections both with the saltwater ocean and with fresh water draining off the land. This happens where a river meets the sea.

The saltiness of estuarine water changes twice daily as saltwater tides flow up the estuary. It also changes when rain falls upriver and fresh water flows through the estuary to the sea, diluting the salt water.

Estuaries usually have calm water. They provide many sorts of habitats and are rich in life forms. However, estuarine plants and animals need to be able to cope with changes in water salinity, temperature and light levels.

Humans use estuaries as harbours, fishing grounds and housing sites. The development of estuarine shores means loss of natural habitats and possible pollution of the water.

ESTUARIES

The river estuary at the top of the picture is connected to the sea by a channel through the sandbar.

Humans and seabirds fish the rich waters of estuaries.

Estuarine mudflats provide habitat for wading birds.

DELTAS AND BARS

As water flows down a river to the sea, it carries a load of sediment. When it reaches the sea, it is slowed down and drops its load. First it drops coarser sand and grit, then it drops finer sand and mud. The sediments may spread out to form a delta, a triangular piece of land through which the river flows in several channels. As the river finally enters the ocean, it may drop sand or mud to form a bar.

At high tide, the sea washes over the sandbar and floods this tidal creek.

A big sandbar that has become sand dunes.

Estuaries

WHERE RIVERS MEET SEAS

ESTUARY LIFE

Herons and other waterbirds fish along banks and creeks and in mangroves.

Dolphins and sharks find plenty of fish in estuary waters.

Sea-eagles catch fish from the surface of the estuary.

The Estuarine Catfish uses its fleshy whiskers to feel for food in sand or mud.

Fish fry grow large enough to survive the open sea in the shelter of the estuary.

Many bottom-living fishes hunt crabs and molluscs on the estuary floor.

Estuaries support many life forms but are not rich in species diversity. Nutrients come into the estuary from both the sea and the land. The shallow water lets light filter through it to make plants grow. However, only species that can cope with estuarine salinity levels, temperatures and changing water levels survive.

FACTS 'N' FIGURES FILE

- **Estuaries are claimed** to be the sites of the most productive natural ecosystems[G] on Earth.

- **Estuaries are rich in phytoplankton,** tiny plants that drift with the tides. These form food for fish fry and other creatures.

- **The temperature** in shallow estuary water when the tide is out may rise to over 50°C. When the tide rushes back into the estuary, the temperature drops suddenly.

- **Plant material** falling into an estuary is broken down by bacteria into nutrients for more plant growth.

- **Conditions are often tough** for estuarine life forms. They may be smaller or have shorter life spans than relatives living in marine or freshwater habitats.

- **Salinity levels** vary greatly within an estuary. Some life forms can survive widely varying salinity levels, others can't.

- **Some species spend** only part of their life cycle in an estuary. When mature, they drift or swim to the open sea.

- **Many estuarine animals** burrow into mud or sand for protection. Bottom-feeding animals are often camouflaged.

- **Seagrass beds,** which provide food for Dugong, turtles and other creatures, grow well in estuaries. They are easily damaged by pollution and dredging.

Salt marshes and lagoons

A salt marsh is a coastal habitat that overlaps sea and land. It often has soil made fertile by plant remains. The plants and animals that live in salt marshes must be able to survive saltwater flooding, sometimes twice each 24 hours. When exposed to air, they must be able to survive wide shifts of temperature.

There are more salt marsh areas in southern Australia than in northern Australia. Salt marshes in Tasmania and Victoria may have up to 60 species of plants growing in them. Salt marshes in northern Australia may have only 10 species of plants.

Where sea water is trapped in a lagoon[G] and then evaporates, a coastal salt lake may form.

Salt marshes may be flooded at high tide. They form harsh environments for plants and animals.

When sea water is trapped in a lagoon and cut off from the sea, a coastal salt lake forms.

CREATURES OF SWAMPS AND MARSHES

Large waterbirds such as ibis find food in swamps.

Some salt-tolerant ducks feed in marshes.

Bandicoots visit salt marshes to look for food.

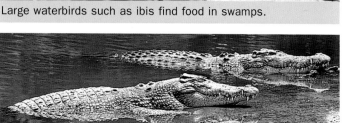

The Saltwater Crocodile is found in northern swamps.

Swamp and marsh animals are a mixture of land and marine species. Crabs and molluscs feed on the algae that live on the surface of the mud. Land animals, such as birds, native rodents[G], bandicoots and snakes, enter salt marshes at low tide. Some are looking for plants to eat, but usually these are too salty. Most visitors are predators looking for prey. Salt marshes are important feeding grounds for migratory[G] wading birds.

Salt marshes and lagoons

MANGROVE SWAMPS

HEADS IN THE AIR, FEET IN THE WATER

Mangroves are salt-tolerant trees that are most common on Australia's northern coasts. They grow along coasts and estuaries and form swampy ecosystems that are home to many species of animals. A mangrove swamp is usually protected from waves. The tides flood it with sea water, but the mangrove trees are never fully submerged.

A mangrove can grow in waterlogged ground because it puts up special breathing roots that take oxygen from the air. Sometimes these roots grow from the trunk and lower branches and help prop the mangrove in place.

A mangrove filters out some salt from the water it takes in. It gets rid of more salt through its leaves. Salt is also stored in the leaves, which fall off, taking the salt with them.

Mangrove swamps fix coastal sand and mud in place. They protect important breeding grounds for many fish species and invertebrate animals.

Mangrove fruits.

Mangrove tree with aerating roots.

Mangrove seedlings.

Fallen leaves contain salt.

FACTS 'N' FIGURES FILE

• **Northern Australia** has around 35 species of mangroves. Central New South Wales has two species. One species grows at a few places along the southern coastline.

• **Molluscs that feed** on the mud at low tide often climb mangrove trees to escape the incoming water.

• **Water passed out by mangrove** leaves evaporates, leaving crystals of salt on the leaf surfaces.

• **Mangroves growing in South Australia's** Gulf St Vincent form swamps that may move as much as 18 m per year. They may spread onto mudflats, or retreat from drying land.

• **As mangrove swamps are destroyed,** fish stocks decrease, destroying commercial and sporting fisheries.

• **Humans discharge waste water** that contains sewage, fertilisers, detergents and heavy metals. Mangrove swamps use up some of these things and help make others less harmful.

• **The rush by Australians to live by the sea** means that mangroves and salt marshes are under threat along much of the continent's coastline.

• **Salt marshes and mangroves** are good habitat for mosquitoes and sandflies. When humans spray these places with pesticide, other creatures are killed as well.

OLDEST ON EARTH

These rocky stromatolites grow in a salt lagoon in Shark Bay, Western Australia. They are made up of layers of sediment and cyanobacteria, a simple form of life whose ancestors grew in Earth's seas 3500 million years ago.

Soft bottom habitats

Soft bottom habitats are sandy or muddy seabeds that are never exposed to the air. Around Australian coasts, they are found from the low-tide mark to the edge of the continental shelf. This is the gently sloping area that stretches from the border of a landmass out to sea to a depth of 150–200 m. Soft bottom habitats form where this shelf is covered with sediment.

Most large creatures that make their homes in soft bottom habitats live just under the surface or on the surface of the sediment. Animals that burrow deeper must be small and move slowly through the thick sediment. Some very small creatures live in the water-filled spaces between sediment grains. Even tinier organisms exist on the surfaces of sediment particles.

CREATURES OF THE SOFT SEABED

Scallops open their shells to filter out food from the incoming tide.

A sea cucumber eats sand or mud and digests the food material in it.

A sea pen is a colony of filter-feeders.

Cones spear worms, other molluscs and even small fish with poison darts.

The Eastern Stargazer sucks prey into its huge mouth.

Pufferfishes have poison in skins and organs.

Fish that live on soft bottoms often have bulging eyes on top of their heads.

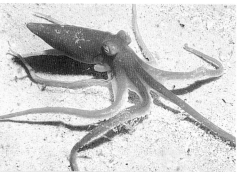
This octopus is hunting for crabs across a sandflat.

Slipper lobsters have flattened feelers.

Soft bottom habitats

SUBMERGED MUD AND SAND

CAMOUFLAGE HELPS SURVIVAL

Some crabs use their claws to hook algae or sponges onto their shells.

The pattern on this ray's skin blends with its surroundings.

A sea urchin hides by spiking seabed debris on its spines.

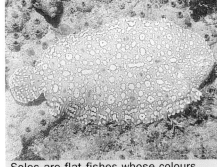

Soles are flat fishes whose colours match the seabed.

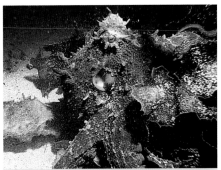

Octopuses can change colour to match their surroundings.

COMMENSALS

The Giant Sand Star (above) eats molluscs. A tiny crab (arrowed right) lives amongst the sand star's sucking tube feet, eating scraps of prey. This interaction, which helps one animal and does not affect the other one, is called commensalism.

SHIFTING SANDS

Sandbanks can be swept away by currents and laid down somewhere else. The sandbanks shown here are protected from the open ocean by an offshore island.

Seagrass beds

Seagrasses are flowering plants that, millions of years ago, became adapted to life under the sea. Most seagrasses have long, strap-like leaves, though one Australian species has rounded leaves. These plants are found growing in sandy sediment, in calm water, from mid-tide level to well below low-tide level. If the water is clear, they can grow at depths of more than 10 m.

Seagrasses hold down sediment, provide shade, help keep water temperatures even, and offer surfaces to which life forms can attach themselves. Seagrass meadows also provide food for animals ranging from bacteria and sponges to sea stars, fishes, turtles and the Dugong.

A sea star in oarweed, a type of seagrass with rounded leaves.

The Dugong is a marine mammal that eats only seagrasses.

Dead seagrass may form mats up to 2 m thick on southern beaches. These piles of rotting plants are home to amphipods, worms and many other creatures.

SEAHORSES

The seahorse is a fish. Its skin carries bony plates.

The male seahorse looks after the eggs.

Seahorses curl their tails around seagrass stems to anchor themselves. The female seahorse passes her eggs to the male, which keeps them in his belly pouch until they hatch. Then he gives birth to the babies.

SEADRAGONS

The seadragon is a relative of the seahorse.

A male seadragon's tail with eggs on its underside.

Seadragons (like this Weedy Seadragon) may be camouflaged by streamers that make them look like seaweed. The male takes the female's eggs into special pockets under his tail. They stay there until they hatch.

Seaweeds

While seagrasses are land plants that have adapted to life in the ocean, seaweeds first grew in the ocean and have remained there.

A seaweed has no roots, stem, branches, leaves or flowers. Its separate parts are called fronds and it sticks itself in one place with a disc called a holdfast. Some seaweeds can survive regular exposure to air at low tides.

Seaweeds get food materials and oxygen from the water. Like land plants, they need sunlight for food-making by photosynthesis.

Seaweeds are also called marine algae. They are divided into blue-green algae and green algae (found at higher levels), brown algae (growing at medium depths), and red algae (growing at greater depths where the light is much less).

THE SEAWEED STORY

This grapeweed, or Neptune's necklace, looks green but is really a brown alga.

Blue-green algae can survive out of water for some time.

Bull-kelp is a strong brown alga found in southern waters.

Two species of green alga. Green algae grow where plenty of sunlight reaches them.

Red algae can grow at water depths that get less sunlight.

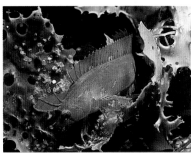

Weedfishes have special fins that cling to seaweed fronds.

FACTS 'N' FIGURES FILE

• **Seagrasses are related** to land grasses. The pollen from their simple flowers is carried to others by currents.

• **Seagrasses can produce** young plants that develop roots while still attached to their parent. When old enough, they break away and take root in the sediment.

• **Balls of seagrass fibres** rolled up by the waves may be found along southern beaches. They can be 30 cm in diameter.

• **Seahorses and seadragons** have long, tube-like snouts. They suck in tiny creatures like sucking through a straw.

• **Seaweeds are more nutritious** than seagrasses.

• **Seaweeds need firm surfaces** for attaching their holdfasts.

• **South Australia** and southern Western Australia have the highest number of seaweed species.

• **A dense bed of kelp** produces as much plant material (about 2 kg/m^2 per year) as high-yielding grassland.

• **When attacked** by grazing creatures, some tropical green and brown algae can change chemicals in their fronds from non-toxic^G to toxic forms.

• **Seaweed beds are home** to many fish species. Some of these fishes are camouflaged so they blend with the weed.

Rocky shores

Rocky shores are littered with stones and boulders. They slope down to rocky reefs that may be partly uncovered at low tide. Sometimes a rocky beach lies between rocky headlands. Sometimes its rocks stand in sand.

Rocky shore plants and animals must have ways of clinging to rock surfaces in order to resist crashing waves. Those at higher levels must survive periods exposed to the air and the Sun. There is fierce competition amongst organisms of one species for the best places to attach and to obtain exposure to water that carries food and oxygen.

SHORELINES OF STONE

A rocky shore on the southern coastline of Australia.

A rock platform and rock pools exposed at low tide.

A beach made up of rocks and sand.

Waves battering lower levels of a rocky coast.

Rocky shores

ZONES OF A ROCKY COAST

ABOVE-TIDAL ZONE – KEPT MOIST BY SPRAY

Periwinkle black zone: Blue-green algae may make the rock look black. Snail-like molluscs (periwinkles), limpets and small crustaceans cling to rocks. Fast-moving crabs and amphipods shelter under rocks.

HIGH INTERTIDAL ZONE – UNDER WATER ONLY AT HIGH TIDE

Barnacle zone: Barnacles are protected by shell plates and filter-feed when the tide is in. Other life includes small snail-like molluscs that feed on brown algae, limpets, sea stars, sea anemones and crabs.

LOW INTERTIDAL ZONE – UNDER WATER FOR MOST OF THE TIDE CYCLE

Cunjevoi zone: Cunjevoi look like plants but are animals (ascidians or sea squirts). Molluscs, sea urchins, crabs, sea lettuce and worms that live in hard, white tubes and filter-feed when waves wash over also live here.

BELOW-TIDAL ZONE – SOMETIMES EXPOSED AT EXTREME LOW TIDE

Seaweed zone: Covered by water most of the time. Its life forms cannot survive being exposed to air too often or too long. There are many seaweeds and molluscs in this zone as well as various marine animals.

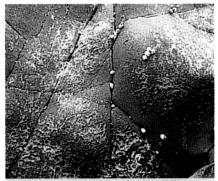

Algae provide grazing for snail-like molluscs in higher tidal zones.

Barnacles filter-feed when the tide covers the zone they live in.

ROCKY COAST RESIDENTS

This abalone's muscular foot forms a vacuum^G seal to hold it on the rock.

Limpets and snail-like molluscs graze on algae on the rocks and in the pools.

Sea stars roam the rock pools on the tiny tube feet under their multiple arms.

FACTS 'N' FIGURES FILE

- **Some sea urchins on rocky shores** bore holes into the rock. They jam themselves into the holes with tube feet and spines.

- **Thick shells** keep the bodies of many shore animals from drying out. The shells also protect them against predators.

- **Many rocky shore creatures** are camouflaged. One crab encourages algae and sponges to grow on its shell.

- **Sea stars** move up and down the rocks with the tide, hunting molluscs.

- **The octopus hunts** tidal pools in search of crabs to eat. It can change colour to match its surroundings.

- **Molluscs on rocky shores** are usually one-shelled gastropods^G. They hold on with a muscular foot that forms a vacuum seal with the rock.

- **In higher zones,** rock-dwellers have to survive harsh conditions. Further down the shore, they have to survive predators and competitors for food and space.

- **A creature that clings** to a rock face usually has a streamlined shape so that water cannot catch it and drag it away.

- **Life forms on rocky shores** have to survive harsh conditions at high levels and predators and competitors lower down.

- **Seaweeds** that grow on rocky coasts are either large and leafy with strong holdfasts, or small, mat-like species.

- **Rock pools** form good habitats if they remain cool and are flushed by the tide.

Rocky reefs

Rocky shores slope down to rocky reefs. Where the ocean temperature is above 16°C, these reefs may become covered with coral. In cooler seas around southern Australia, the rocks become covered with seaweeds and invertebrate animals. Rocky reefs are rich in biodiversity[G].

Many of the invertebrate animals of a rocky reef live in colonies[G]. Sponges, ascidians, bryozoans and coral colonies are all made up of similar individuals. A colony grows bigger by adding extra units.

Life on a rocky reef can be crowded, and there is fierce competition for the best sites. Many invertebrates defend themselves and some attack their competitors.

If an area of rock becomes bare, surrounding colonial invertebrates quickly add on more units and spread over the space. Tiny larval animals drift onto the bare spot and settle. Algae grow there, and are grazed by molluscs and other herbivores. Soon the place looks like the rest of the reef.

ROCKY REEFS

Part of this rocky reef is exposed at low tide. Part remains submerged. Different creatures live in each part.

A rocky reef extends into the sea below a rocky shore and line of cliffs.

FACTS 'N' FIGURES FILE

- **Some sea anemones** have defensive tentacles armed with stinging cells.

- **Rock lobsters** have been found feeding on barnacles and mussels whose hard shells protect them from most predators.

- **There are more small spaces** on a rocky reef than large spaces. Large creatures have to fight hard to get a home.

- **The diversity of animals** on a rocky reef depends on the number of holes available.

- **Gastropod molluscs** use a rasp-like tongue called a radula to get food. They may rasp off pieces of rock to get algae.

- **Some sponges and ascidians** produce chemicals that stop other creatures settling on them. Scientists have studied these creatures, hoping they may discover new anti-fouling[G] paints for ships.

- **The word cephalopod** means "head-foot". Octopus and squid appear to be all head and tentacles.

- **An octopus stranded** in a rock pool can crawl across the rocks using its arms. In the water, it jets along by squirting water.

Rocky reefs

NEIGHBOURS

Each creature tries to preserve its own living space by using force, chemical means or overgrowing others.

Predatory fishes, such as this Green Moray Eel, have regular hunting territories.

Many rock and reef species are fixed in place or move very slowly. In order to get living space, they may overgrow their neighbours, or give out chemicals that poison them. They may defend themselves with sharp spines, stinging tentacles or slimy mucus[G]. Some shed surface tissue so that overgrowing organisms cannot take hold.

Fishes may defend one part of a reef as a place to shelter, feed and breed. Many species have special ways of behaving, called displays, that tell other fishes of the same sort that the displaying fish claims this territory.

CONTINENTAL OFFCUTS

A continental island is a mountain peak that was once part of the mainland, but has been cut off by rising seas. Some rocky islands are the tips of extinct volcanoes. In cooler seas these islands will be surrounded by rocky reefs. In the tropics, coral reefs will fringe them.

Right: One of the Whitsunday Group of continental islands.

COLOUR ME CUTTLE

Cephalopods include octopus, squid and cuttles. They are molluscs with many arms and a large head containing the internal organs. They have good eyesight and the most advanced nervous system of all invertebrates. They can change colour when hunting, hiding or interacting with others.

Three cuttle colour-changes. A cuttle has ten appendages[G] surrounding its mouth.

Coral reefs

Coral polyps are tiny, fragile marine invertebrates that live in clear, warm, shallow seas. Their hollow bodies have a mouth at one end, which is surrounded by stinging tentacles.

Many coral polyps have algae called zooxanthellae growing in their tissues. These use sunlight and the waste products of the coral polyp to make oxygen and food that can be used by the polyp.

Each polyp takes lime from sea water and builds itself a hard case. Some coral polyps live alone, but many live in colonies. When a coral polyp dies, a new polyp builds its case over it. The colony expands and gradually a coral reef builds up. Algae, sponges and many other invertebrates grow on the corals, and creatures of many sorts make their homes in and around the coral reef.

ON A CORAL REEF

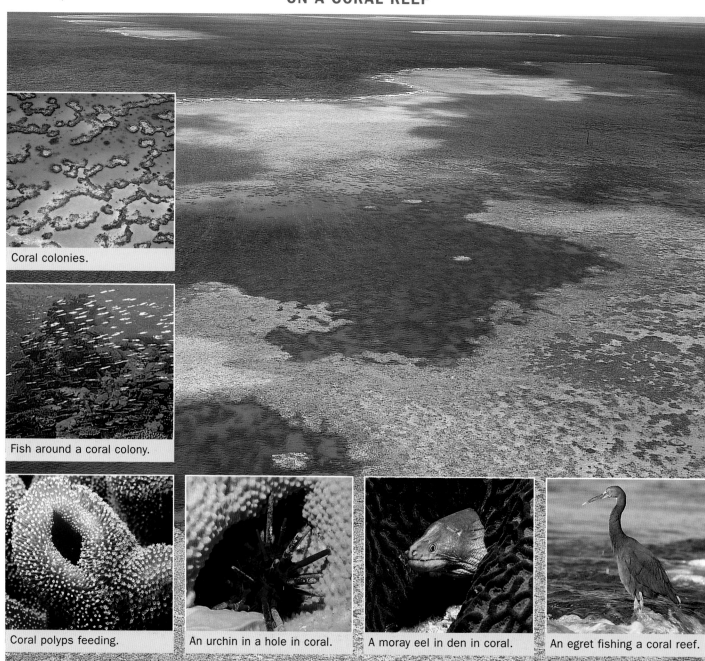

Coral colonies.

Fish around a coral colony.

Coral polyps feeding.

An urchin in a hole in coral.

A moray eel in den in coral.

An egret fishing a coral reef.

Coral reefs

CORAL REEF INTERACTIONS

Crabs may shelter under a sea anemone's stinging tentacles.

Anemonefish make themselves immune[G] to the stings of their sea-anemone home.

Two cleanerfish at work, nipping parasites[G] and dead skin off a cod.

Mobile species camouflage themselves on non-mobile species.

In a coral reef, many different species of animals are crowded together. Some graze algae; some filter food from sea water or sediment; some are predators. Coral reef species can interact. Symbionts are creatures that live closely together in a relationship that benefits at least one of them (symbiosis = living together).

This species of spindle cowrie is found only on gorgonian corals.

FACTS 'N' FIGURES FILE

- **Coral reefs** have existed on Earth for over 400 million years.

- **Corals grow** where sea temperatures range from 18 to 30°C. They need clear water so that the zooxanthellae living in their polyps can use sunlight to make food by photosynthesis.

- **The association between** coral polyp and zooxanthellae benefits both parties.

- **An anemonefish** cannot survive without an anemone. Its skin makes mucus that protects it against the stings of its anemone home.

- **Coral that is stressed** by rising water temperatures may expel its zooxanthellae. This bleaches the coral, which eventually dies.

- **Many coral reef fishes** are territorial. A male damselfish 15 cm long will attack a human diver who swims too near its eggs.

- **Cleaner fishes** advertise their services by doing special displays at "cleaning stations".

DIFFERENT DINERS, DIFFERENT DINNERS

The butterflyfish probes coral for invertebrates.

The cowfish blows sand from seabed prey.

The damselfish grazes on algae.

The lionfish hunts shrimps on the seabed.

Snapper hunt small fishes at night.

The trumpetfish sucks prey into its snout.

A small area of coral reef can be home to many different sorts of fishes. This is because many of them eat different things and shelter in different places. Two species that eat the same food may have different ways of getting it, so they use different niches, or mini-habitats, in the reef.

Coral cays and atolls

Coral grows in shallow sea where light reaches it. Where a reef grows well, it will build upwards towards the surface. Waves break pieces from the crest of the reef and this coral rubble and sand and broken shells lodge on top of the reef. Eventually a coral cay, whose crown is above the high tide mark, is formed.

Seabirds roost and nest on the cay and their droppings break down to form fertile soil. Plant seeds drift or blow onto the cay, or are carried by birds, and the cay becomes a vegetated coral island.

The shallow water near a coral cay is called the reef flat. A fringing reef grows on this area. The reef flat is protected by the seaward crest of the reef, which takes the force of the waves.

An atoll is an island in the form of a ring, or part of a ring, around a piece of water called a lagoon. Atolls form where coral grows upwards on the rims of extinct volcanoes that are very slowly sinking into the sea.

A VIEW OF A CORAL CAY

A coral cay (top right) surrounded by its reef flat and fringing reef. The crest of the reef encircles the reef flat.

Life on the reef flat of a coral cay at high tide.

Coral rubble is made up of broken coral and shells.

Terns roost and nest on the coral rubble on the shore of a cay.

A vegetated coral cay and a bare cay separated by a channel.

Coral cays and atolls

ISLANDS OF CORAL

BIRDS OF THE CORAL SEAS

Boobies nest on coral islands.

Tropicbirds nest on the island shore.

Terns nest in colonies on cays.

Shearwaters nest in island burrows.

Seabirds roost and nest on coral cays and islands. Migratory shorebirds rest and feed there before flying to their next feeding ground. A few land birds live there once the plant cover is thick enough for them to feed and nest in.

SEEDS OF LIFE AND DEATH

A noddy preening[G] Pisonia seeds from its feathers. Inset: Noddies on nest.

Plants that grow on coral cays must spread their seeds. The Pisonia tree is a favourite nesting site for noddies. Its seeds stick to a bird's feathers and are carried away. The bird can become hopelessly tangled in the seeds. It cannot fly and starves to death.

LIFE CYCLE OF MARINE TURTLES

After mating, a female turtle drags herself above high-tide level.

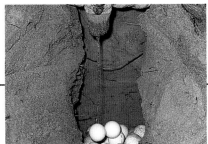
She scoops a nest chamber and lays her eggs in it.

She covers the eggs with sand.

Then she goes back to sea.

Tiny turtles hatch. They dig to the surface of the sand.

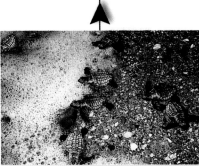
They dash across the beach to the sea and swim away.

The open ocean

The temperature and salinity of the surface layers of the open ocean stay fairly even.

Where there are suitable nutrients, the surface waters contain countless numbers of drifting, single-celled plants and animals. Cold currents travelling towards the Equator carry more nutrients and contain more plankton that do warmer currents flowing away from the Equator. Larger, multi-celled, swimming animals feed on the

plankton. In turn, these larger creatures are eaten by still larger ones.

As depth in the ocean increases, less and less light gets through until the water is dark. The temperature gets colder and pressure increases. Life forms exist at all levels, from the surface right down to the deepest trench, 11 000 m below. Here the pressure is 1000 times more than that at the surface and the temperature is just above freezing.

OPEN OCEAN CONNECTIONS

Plankton drift in the currents.

Schools of small fishes eat plankton.

Seabirds eat small fishes.

Sea jellies eat plankton.

Dolphins eat fishes. Their body wastes and remains release nutrients used by plankton.

Large fishes eat smaller fishes. They are eaten by other predators.

Turtles eat sea jellies.

The seabed creatures shown at right depend for food upon nutrients sinking from the surface. These nutrients include animal body wastes and carcasses.

Brittle star.

Sea pens and nudibranchs.

Sea anemone.

The open ocean

IN THE DEEP BLUE SEA

THE BIG ONES

Whale Shark.

Manta Ray.

Southern Right Whales.

Humpback Whales.

These giants feed on tiny drifting plankton or on small crustaceans known as krill. They take in huge amounts to fuel their enormous bodies. The Whale Shark and Manta Ray are fishes; whales are marine mammals.

FACTS 'N' FIGURES FILE

- **Pelagic species** are those that live in the open sea.

- **Benthic species** live on the seabed.

- **In El Niño**[G] **years,** cool ocean currents flow along the coast of eastern Australia. Fish catches are good.

- **In La Niña**[G] **years,** warm currents lower ocean nutrient levels off eastern Australia. Fish catches decline.

- **Deep sea creatures** are carnivores.

Many have enormous mouths and some have body-lights to attract prey or mates.

- **The Whale Shark** may grow to 12 m long. It filters plankton through its gill slits.

- **The Manta Ray** may grow to 7 m across its "wings".

- **A Humpback Whale** may grow to 15 m in length and may weigh 65 t.

- **A Southern Right Whale** may grow to 17 m long and may weigh 85 t.

- **Countershading** (dark backs, pale bellies) camouflages pelagic fishes.

- **Most deep seabed creatures** eat dead material that falls from the surface.

- **Underwater volcanic vents** jet lava[G] and chemicals into the deep sea. Bacteria make energy from the chemicals. The bacteria support a food web that includes tube worms, crabs, shrimps and other creatures.

Interacting with the oceans

Worldwide, the areas along the seashores of the continents are the most heavily populated.

In Australia, the most popular place to live, work and have fun is on the coast. Industry sets up factories on the coast, where it is cheaper to ship in raw materials and ship out finished goods.

Farmers grow crops and pasture dairy cattle and other animals where rivers have dropped fertile soil when their flow slows to enter the sea.

Estuaries are harbours for fishing fleets.

Beaches and islands are bordered with holidaymakers.

Human pressures on shores, estuaries and coastal waters are growing all the time.

PRESSURES ON COAST AND OCEAN

- Sewage and industrial waste dumped in the ocean pollute it with excess nutrients, bacteria and poisons.
- Oil spills smother and poison marine life.
- Agricultural chemicals and fertilisers pollute the sea.
- Rubbish dumped at sea chokes and traps seabirds and marine creatures such as turtles.
- Abandoned fishing nets kill animals.
- Over-harvesting has destroyed some fish stocks.
- Coral and shell collecting destroy invertebrates.
- Whales are still killed by some countries.
- Tourists and holidaymakers may harm corals and other ecosystems.
- Nuclear waste dumping is dangerous.
- Development of shores leads to destruction of mangroves and mudflats.
- Four-wheel-drive vehicles can harm sand dunes and beaches, and the creatures that live there.

Australians are increasingly moving to the coast.

Beaches are used as playgrounds and highways.

Fishing fleets have increasingly efficient ways of catching fish.

Danger!

SHARKS IN THEIR ELEMENT

Worldwide, each year, about 70–100 shark attacks on humans are reported. These attacks result in 5–15 reported deaths.

Most attacks occur in shallow water near shore, often inshore of a sandbar where sharks are trapped at low tide, or near steep drop-offs where they feed on fish.

The species that most regularly attack humans are the Great White Shark, the Tiger Shark and the Bull Shark. All reach large sizes and normally eat marine mammals, turtles and large fishes.

A shark may attack in one of three ways:
• **A hit and run attack,** usually in the surf zone. The victim seldom sees the shark and it swims away after one slashing bite. It has probably decided the victim is not suitable prey.
• **A bump and bite attack,** usually on a diver or swimmer in deeper water, results in more deaths. A shark hunting prey to eat circles and often bumps the victim before attacking.
• **Sneak attacks** happen without warning. Like bump and bite attacks, the shark returns to bite again: injuries are severe and often kill.

There is less risk of being attacked by a shark if you:
• **Stay in a group and do not wander far from shore.**
• **Avoid swimming at night, dusk or dawn, when sharks are most active.**
• **Do not enter the water if you are bleeding.**
• **Do not wear shiny jewellery that could look like fish scales.**
• **Do not swim near sewage or rubbish outlets.**
• **Do not splash the water or swim with pets.**
• **Take care between sandbars, near drop-offs and in murky water.**
• **Do not enter the water where sharks are being fed (above).**

STAY AWAY FROM THESE

Sea snake.

Lionfish.

Blue-ringed Octopus.

Cone shell.

Marine creatures that can harm or kill humans include sea snakes, the Blue-ringed Octopus and a number of sea jellies, including the Box Jellyfish and the Irukandji. A number of cone shells have venomous stings. The fins of some fishes carry spines that force venom into any wound they make.

FACTS 'N' FIGURES FILE

• **Numbers of shark attacks** are going up each year because of the increasing number of swimmers in the water.

• **Almost any shark** over 2 m in length is a threat to humans.

• **From 1791 to 2000,** Australia had 323 confirmed, unprovoked attacks by sharks. Of these, 152 were fatal (the last in 2000).

• **From 1580 to 2000,** there were 254 attacks by Great White Sharks reported worldwide. Of these, 67 killed the victim.

• **The Great White Shark** is an endangered species. Due to hunting by humans, many shark species are declining in numbers.

• **Sea snakes** do not attack humans, but in the mating season they become fascinated by air hoses and can pester divers. Their venom can kill humans, but most people who are bitten recover.

• **Box jellyfish stings** have killed 55 people in the Indo-Pacific region since 1984. Vinegar makes the sting harmless.

• **The Blue-ringed Octopus** will bite if picked up or trodden on. One octopus weighing 26 g has enough venom to paralyse up to 10 adult humans.

• **Venomous fish** and stingray wounds are very painful. If a piece of the spine carrying the venom stays in the wound, it may become infected.

Spoiling the oceans

Life on Earth began in the ocean. The sea helps make Earth a living planet.

The human population of the world is over 6137 million and increasing. Most of these people live in coastal areas and along the estuaries of major rivers that flow into the sea. Marine creatures have traditionally provided human food, and today's fishing fleets use modern technology in their operations. Many places where fish were plentiful have been fished out. Some methods of fishing, such as long-lining and trawling, kill many animals besides fish.

Seaboard countries claim the sea for 200 nautical miles from their low-tide marks. The rest is international waters. Theoretically, all nations should care for these, but many countries see them as places to grab what fish and other useful things they can, and to dispose of wastes.

TOO MUCH NUTRIENT

Algae growing in an estuary.

Algae and bacteria form a sludgy coating on plants.

Human, industrial and agricultural wastes put extra, unneeded nutrients into freshwater and marine ecosystems. Blue-green algae grow, die and poison other plants as they rot.

OIL SPILLS

Wrecks and accidents discharge oil.

Oil spills kill many sorts of marine animals.

The petroleum industry has a good safety record in Australian waters. Not all countries have the same high safety standards for oil tankers they register.

WE'RE SWIMMING IN IT!

In 1999, the World Wide Fund for Nature released a Marine Pollution Report Card that named Australia's marine "hot spots":

• **Sydney sewerage system,** NSW – nearly all Sydney's sewerage is discharged directly into the ocean. The three main outlets discharge over 5 000 000 000 L of sewage (enough to fill 2000 Olympic swimming pools) into the ocean every day. This sewage has been given only a low level of treatment (not acceptable in other States).

• **Acid seepage into estuaries,** NSW – seepage from cleared soils carries acid into waterways and kills marine life.

• **Western Port Bay,** V – greatly altered by sediment, pollution and agricultural run-off. Seventy industries are licensed to discharge wastes into the bay. Eighty-five per cent of the seagrass beds have been destroyed.

• **Introduced pests,** all States – about 130 species have been introduced, mostly in discharged ballast[G] water.

• **Tributyltin (TBT),** all States – TBT is a toxin painted onto boat hulls to stop marine organisms attaching themselves. It harms marine creatures such as oysters and scallops, and is passed up the food chain to seals, dolphins and humans.

• **Agricultural run-off,** Q – the Great Barrier Reef's corals and other life are threatened by sediment and fertilisers.

• **Estuary pollution,** all States – all around Australia's coasts estuaries are in poor condition from agricultural run-off, stormwater and sewage discharge, land clearing and mangrove clearing. Pollution destroys seagrass beds.

• **Marine litter,** all States – only Tasmania has surveyed marine litter. On average, each kilometre of Tasmanian beach had 300 items of litter. Much of it was from the fishing industry. Marine litter kills seals, sea-lions, dolphins, whales and seabirds.

• **Industrial pollution,** T – the Derwent and Tamar estuaries are polluted by pulp and paper mill wastes. Macquarie Harbour is polluted by wastes from mining.

Harming marine environments

POLLUTION

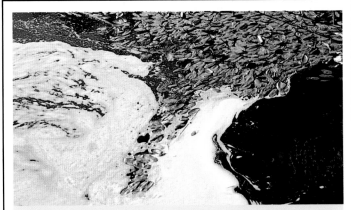

Pollution pouring into a river will end up in the sea.

Chemicals used by agriculture and industry pour into the ocean in many places. Some kill marine organisms. Some unbalance marine environments by flooding them with nutrients. Some harm the reproduction[G] of plants and animals. Some may cause diseases such as cancer. The animals affected by chemicals may have some place in food chains that end up on human dining tables.

GLOBAL WARMING

The ocean acts like a sponge, soaking up heat. At present, global temperatures are rising. Human activity, such as burning fossil fuels[G], contributes to this. A small rise in sea temperatures harms the zooplankton that are vital to the oceanic food chains. Warming water can also cause corals to expel the algae that help them make food. The corals bleach, then die.

The Sun's heat warms the sea.

RADIOACTIVE DUMPING

Radioactive[G] wastes were dumped into the sea by many nations from 1946 to 1993. Huge amounts of spent fuels and liquid waste from nuclear reactors, and even "hot" parts from reactors, have been dropped and poured into the ocean. Much of this waste was in containers that have rusted or broken. Animals that live near dumping sites carry large amounts of radioactivity in their bodies. Research continues on whether radioactive poisons can be passed up the food chain to humans who eat seafood.

INTRODUCED PESTS

Since 1770, many ships have visited Australia. Some have brought foreign creatures on their hulls; some have carried water in their cargo holds. This, and any pests that it held, used to be discharged in Australian waters. Some marine pests have entered our seas with imported live food species, such as oysters. One tiny organism causes paralytic shellfish poisoning in vertebrates, such as humans, eating affected mussels and oysters.

FACTS 'N' FIGURES FILE

- **Between 1951 and 1993,** ocean waters off California, USA, rose in temperature up to 1.6°C. Numbers of zooplankton dropped by 80% and commercial fish catches fell by 30%.

- **The ocean holds heat.** While an inland area may vary up to 30°C between day and night, the sea's surface varies only a few degrees at most.

- **It is uncertain how much global warming** is due to human activities and how much to the Earth's climatic swings.

- **A report published in 1991** noted that, over 45 years, at least 12 nations had dumped radioactive wastes at 73 different sites around the world's oceans.

- **In 1993, the USA** and 36 other governments voted to ban dumping radioactive material at sea. Nations that did not sign the ban included Britain, France, China, Belgium and Russia.

- **Radioactive wastes** from British tests in the 1950s were dumped on Queensland, Tasmanian and Northern Territory coasts.

- **The worst oil spill in Australian waters,** in 1991, saw 17 280 t of oil escape when the Greek tanker *Kirki* lost its bow off WA.

- **About 37% of the oil** polluting the sea comes from industrial and human waste material via stormwater drains and sewage.

- **Species introduced in ballast water** include the Northern Pacific Seastar, the Japanese Kelp, the Giant European Fanworm and the Yellowfin Goby. All of these can take over a reef or soft bottom community.

Saving coasts and oceans

WAYS IN WHICH PEOPLE CAN PROTECT THE OCEAN

1 Household sewage and stormwater drains flow into waterways and the ocean, so harsh cleaning agents and chemicals should not be poured down the sink or toilet. Dispose of them in the garbage.

2 Conserve water and avoid overloading the sewerage system, which can overflow into waterways when it rains.

3 Buy organic food if you can. Agricultural chemicals and fertilisers pollute the ocean.

4 Never drop rubbish on a beach. Carry a plastic bag on beach walks to collect rubbish and put it in a garbage bin.

5 If you go fishing, remember that many species are being over-fished. Quickly throw back anything you can't eat.

6 Don't buy marine wildlife products such as coral, sharks' teeth or shells.

7 Don't throw rubbish overboard from a boat. It kills marine life and pollutes beaches.

8 If you explore the seashore and reefs, try not to touch anything and replace any rocks you have shifted.

9 Stay away from colonies of nesting seabirds.

10 Remember that cars running along a beach destroy animal habitats.

○ WHERE TO DRAW LINES IN THE SAND ○

Fraser Island, Q, where Dingos (inset) became dependent on humans for food. Some became dangerous and a boy was killed.

Where dolphins visit humans, efforts are now made to see they keep on hunting their own fish.

Humans like to interact with coastal wildlife. But animals can grow dependent on human hand-outs, which can damage their health or lead to aggression towards people. It is best for wild animals if humans enjoy looking at them but leave them alone rather than feeding them or changing their habitats.

Our coastal heritage

AUSTRALIA'S MARINE PARKS

Fish-watching on Lord Howe Island.

Biosphere Reserves that contain coastal habitats include:
- Prince Regent River Reserve, WA;
- Southwest National Park, T;
- Fitzgerald River National Park, WA;
- Wilsons Promontory National Park, V;
- Croajingolong National Park, V.

At present (September 2001) Australia has 14 places on the World Heritage List. The sites that include important coastal elements are:
- Shark Bay, WA;
- Fraser Island, Q;
- Great Barrier Reef, Q;
- Lord Howe Island Group, NSW;
- Heard and McDonald Islands (410 km south-west of Perth);
- Macquarie Island (1500 km south-east of Tasmania);
- Kakadu National Park, NT.

Commonwealth Marine Protected Areas include:
Ashmore Reef Nature Reserve, Cartier Island Nature Reserve, Coringa–Herald Nature Reserve, Elizabeth and Middleton Reefs, Marine National Nature Reserve, the Great Australian Bight Marine Park, Lihou Reef National Nature Reserve, Mermaid Reef Marine National Nature Reserve, Ningaloo Marine Park, Solitary Islands Marine Reserve and Tasmanian Seamounts Marine Reserve. All are managed by Environment Australia. The Great Barrier Reef Marine Park is managed by the Great Barrier Reef Marine Park Authority.

A WHALE TALE WITH, WE HOPE, A HAPPY ENDING

Whale-watching.

Australia's final whaling station, Cheynes Beach near Albany, WA, closed in 1978, ending 200 years of slaughter for whale oil, baleen and meat. Commercial whaling has been forbidden worldwide since 1986. Some countries, including Japan and Norway, continue to kill whales. In Australia, whale-watching has become a great eco-tourism attraction.

Whales found in Australian waters include:
Humpback – has recovered from 200 in 1965 to around 4 400 off eastern Australia.
Southern right – protected in 1935. In 1990 there were around 300. Today there are probably 1200–1400.
Blue – the largest animal to exist on Earth. Has increased from near extinction to possibly 1300 in southern waters.
Sperm – from 1952 to 1978, Australians killed 16 000 Sperm Whales. Numbers are recovering worldwide.
Minke – still hunted by Japanese whalers "for science".

FACTS 'N' FIGURES FILE

- **The numbers of Humpback Whales** on Australia's east coast increase by 10% per year. However, 4 400 is well below the pre-1939 estimate of 20 000.

- **Australia has two Humpback Whale** populations, on the east and west coasts. East coast male Humpbacks will change their songs to copy strange males who swim in from the west coast.

- **Two kilometres off the coast** at Warrnambool, Victoria, there is a Blue Whale feeding ground where cold water wells up and attracts krill and plankton.

- **Whale-watching base towns** estimate that each Humpback Whale sighted is worth $100 000 to local businesses.

- **The State and Territory Governments** are responsible for marine environments up to 3 nautical miles from their territorial sea baseline, usually low-water mark.

- **Under United Nations Convention** Australia has rights and responsibilities over 16 000 000 km^2 of ocean.

- **Compared to many places in the world,** Australia's coasts and oceans are in quite good condition.

Glossary

Adapted Changed to suit new conditions.

Algae Chlorophyll-containing plants ranging from one-celled to many-celled forms. Includes seaweeds.

Amphipod Small, scavenging crustaceans, sometimes known as sand hoppers.

Anti-fouling Material that stops build-up of marine organisms on ships.

Appendages Any part of the body not part of the main trunk.

Ascidians A group of marine animals that have a nerve cord in free swimming stage, then settle and become invertebrates.

Bacteria Tiny life forms.

Baleen Curtains of fibre in the mouths of some whales, used to filter food from sea water.

Ballast Heavy material carried in a ship's hold to keep it stable.

Biodiversity Diversity of plants and animals.

Bryozoans A group of colonial invertebrate animals that form a lacy network on solid surfaces.

Buffer Something that takes the shock between two opposing forces. A neutral zone between enemies.

Camouflage To make lost to view by matching the background.

Cells The units from which life forms are made.

Climate The general weather conditions of areas through the year.

Coelenterates A group of invertebrate animals whose bodies are made up of two layers of cells enclosing a digestive cavity.

Colonies Animals of the same kind living in close association.

Community A group of plant and animal organisms living together.

Condense To bring to a more solid shape, as gas to liquid.

Conformation Of a landform: the way it is formed; its outline or shape.

Crustaceans A group of ten-legged animals whose bodies are covered with a hard exoskeleton.

Cyanobacteria Single-celled or colonial water-living organisms that can photosynthesise using chlorophyll. Sometimes called blue-green algae.

Debris The remains of anything broken down or destroyed, such as rock fragments.

Detergent Synthetic cleaning agent.

Detritus Any broken-up material; debris.

Diluting Making thinner or weaker by adding water.

Echinoderms A group of invertebrates with five radial divisions to the body and plates under the skin serving as skeleton.

Ecosystem A community of life forms interacting with each other and with the environment in which they live.

El Niño A climate change that happens every 4 or 5 years. The southern Pacific warms quickly, changing winds and currents. It causes drought in eastern Australia.

Endangered Near to disappearing for ever.

Erosion (*verb* **erode**) The process by which the surface of the Earth is worn away.

Equator A great circle around the Earth that is at equal distances from the North and South Poles.

Evaporates Disappears as vapour.

Excrete To pass out as waste from an organic body.

Extinction (*adj.* **extinct**) The state of no longer existing as a lifeform.

Fauna Animal life.

Filter Pass liquid through something that holds back suspended particles.

Flora Plant life.

Flotsam Things found floating on the sea or washed ashore.

Fossil fuels Things that are derived from the remains of prehistoricorganisms and that produce fire, heat or energy; especially coal, oil and natural gas.

Gastropods A group of molluscs that have one shell and move on a gliding foot.

Gravitational pull The force that attracts all bodies; e.g., falling of things towards the centre of the Earth.

Groyne A jetty or wall built into the sea to prevent erosion.

Herbivores Animals that eat plants.

Immune Protected from a disease or other harm.

Introduced Brought to a place where it does not occur naturally.

Invertebrates Animals without backbones.

La Niña The opposite climate effect of El Niño (see above). La Niña brings heavy rain to eastern Australia.

Lagoon An area of shallow water separated from the sea.

Lava Molten rock, usually from deep within the Earth.

Mammals Animals with backbones whose bodies create heat and which have hair on their skins and feed their babies on milk.

Marine Of the sea.

Marsupials A group of mammals whose young ones are born early in their development and may be carried in a pouch.

Microscopic Too small to be seen by the naked eye.

Migratory Moving between one country and another.

Molluscs A group of invertebrate creatures that have soft, unsegmented bodies that are often protected by shells.

Mucus. A thick liquid produced by an organism.

Nectar A sweet substance produced by flowers.

Non-toxic Not poisonous.

Nutrients Things used as food.

Organisms Living things.

Parasites Organisms that live on or in the body of another species (the host), taking nourishment and causing harm.

Pesticides Chemicals for killing animal pests.

Pioneer One of those that enter or settle a region first.

Poles The points at the extreme north and south of Earth's globe.

Pollen The fine, powdery yellow grains that are the male cells of flowering plants.

Pollute (*noun* **pollution**) To make unclean, foul or unhealthy.

Predators Organisms that kill and eat other organisms.

Preen To put feathers in order with the beak.

Primitive Only slightly changed from early types.

Radioactive Emitting radiation.

Reptiles Animals having backbones and scaly skins whose bodies take on the temperature of their surroundings.

Reproduction The producing of a new generation of individuals.

Rodents A group of mammals whose front teeth grow throughout life, continually wearing back to a chisel-edge.

Rubble Rough pieces of broken stone or coral.

Scavenge (*noun* **scavenger**) To eat dead animal or plant material.

Sediment Material deposited by water, air, or ice.

Spawn To shed eggs and sperm, usually into water.

Terrestrial Of the land.

Toxic Poisonous.

Vacuum Space from which air has been removed.

Vapour Something in the form of gas. Sometimes visible, such as fog, mist, steam or smoke.

Vertebrate An animal with a backbone and/or a spinal column.

Volume The size of something, or the amount of space occupied by it, given in cubic units.

Vulnerable At risk of extinction if the present situation changes.

Weather Day to day state of the atmosphere.